THE SPIRIT OF THE
WEST

Text by Ted Barris   Photographs by Dudley Witney

THE SPIRIT OF THE WEST

Text by Ted Barris   **Photographs by Dudley Witney**

CHARTWELL
BOOKS, INC.

Published in the United States by
Chartwell Books
110 Enterprise Avenue
Secaucus, New Jersey
07094

ISBN: 1-55521-178-X

Design: Don Fernley

Typesetting: Computer Composition of
Canada, Inc.

Printed and bound in Hong Kong by
Scanner Art Services, Toronto

Photograph page 1: Where the trail
ends — a disused wagon in a field in
Wyoming.

Pages 2-3: Extreme temperatures and
aridity produce specially-adapted
vegetation in the Arizona desert.

Page 4: Summer grazing near Ridgway, Colorado.

CONTENTS

1
The Beginnings:
THE PUSH WESTWARD

In 1814, a poetic American lawyer named Francis Scott Key witnessed an American garrison defend Fort McHenry from a British attack, and wrote an anthem about "the land of the free, and the home of the brave." In 1880, French-Canadian Calixa Lavallée composed the music to Adolphe-Basile Routhier's lyric line, "our home and native land," for a banquet in Quebec City.

The "Star-Spangled Banner" did not become the official anthem of the United States until 1931, and "O Canada" wasn't designated the national anthem of Canada until 1967. But the words of the anthems make clear, that for both Americans and Canadians, the land has always been part of the national identity.

The bond between North Americans and the land goes back to the most recent ice age, when the oceans receded until a grassy plain connected Asia and North America. This land bridge across the Bering Strait delivered Canada's and America's first immigrants, whom Christopher Columbus later named "Indians."

Opposite page: A group of Blackfoot Indians, in ceremonial dress, photographed in 1901.

Columbus and his crews were followed by waves of explorers, adventurers, traders, and colonists, all of whom were attracted to this New World. At first they charted its coasts and explored its interior in search of a route to the silk and spice riches of the Far East. Then they harvested its fur-bearing animals and excavated its gold. Finally they came to settle on its shores for good. Within the space of a few generations, two nations of newcomers outgrew the land on the edges of the continent, and moved toward its heart. American immigrants were urged to push westward in a nation which was "destined to manifest to mankind the excellence of divine principles, to establish on earth the noblest temple ever dedicated." And immigrants to Canada were building a nation which would "have dominion also from sea to sea, and from the river unto the ends of the earth."

For politicians of that era, the West was the object of that "manifest destiny," and the means to that "dominion from sea to sea." For the immigrant, however, the West was a last chance to find a home. The West was the last frontier. It would be the destination of the last pioneers in the continent's history. Their devotion to the land, belief in its bounty, faith in its forgiveness, and gratitude for its gifts, make up the story of Western settlement and survival . . . the story of the great westward push.

The land lay waiting, untamed, and largely unknown. Getting there was the immigrant's first great challenge. Legendary wagon masters led trains west from the Mississippi and into history. Among the first were Mormon followers of Brigham Young. On a July afternoon in 1847 the master colonizer, and successor to the martyred Joseph Smith, rose from his carriage/sickbed at the mouth of a mountain canyon above the Salt Lake Valley to proclaim: "This is the place." From their last home, at Nauvoo, Illinois, Young had led an advance party of 143 men, three women, and two children in seventy-two covered wagons 1,400 miles over the trackless Great Plains. Thousands would follow in one of the epic folk movements of American history. Why? For a promised land.

That was the vision of the Reverend Isaac Barr, a British colonizer who, in 1902, convinced 2,000 followers to abandon the "populous and smoky" cities of Britain for "homesteads in the picturesque parklands" of the Canadian Northwest. The immigrants journeyed for weeks aboard a Boer War troopship, were then crowded into primitive train cars, and ended by pushing wagons west through slough and mire. Finally, they straggled onto a limitless prairie,

Mounted Indians await royalty at the turn of the century
near Calgary, Alberta.

scorched by prairie fire, bald, treeless, and flat. Their picture of
paradise was dashed, but their dream of owning land was fulfilled in
the farmlands of Saskatchewan and Alberta.

What drew the Mormons and the Barr Colonists — and millions of
others — to the West, was the chance to hold clear title to a parcel of
land. President Abraham Lincoln offered land for free in the Homestead Act of 1862. Any settler could earn clear title to 160 acres of land
provided he worked it for five years.

Nineteenth-century immigrants were invited to settle in the new world
in booklets like this one, distributed in Holland, in 1884.

This train brought settlers from Colorado to central Alberta in the early years of the twentieth century.

The American bureaucracy called potential settlement areas "Unassigned Lands." On April 22, 1889, the heart of Oklahoma territory was taken from Cherokee, Seminole, Choctaw, Creek and Chickasaw Indians, and opened up to white settlement. Young settlers surrounded the territory. Federal troops patrolled the boundary until a cannon was fired at noon. On foot, on racehorse, in sulky and farm wagon, the "boomers" rushed to mark out their homesteads. They increased the white population of central Oklahoma from zero to 20,000 in one day. Life in the frontier territory was hectic and difficult. In the streets of Tulsey Town (later Tulsa), for example, settlers were forced "to dodge roaming hogs, goats, and cows when

A team of oxen provides the power for breaking grass sod in 1911.

crossing, and sometimes wild animals would venture into the middle of town."

When Clifford Sifton took office as the Canadian Minister of the Interior in 1896, settlement of the western territories of Canada was the priority. Land wasn't free, but it was the cheapest in the world at the turn of the century. Homesteaders on the prairies got 160 acres clear title for ten dollars, provided they cleared ten acres a year for three years, and lived on the holding for six months of the year.

On paper it was simple. In practice, homesteading was an ordeal. For Swedish immigrants who had never seen mosquitoes, plowing required three workers: one to guide the horse team and two waving cloths to keep the horses from being driven to distraction by the swarms of mosquitoes. There was the Saskatchewan homesteader

Homesteaders, their wagons loaded with all their worldly possessions, heeded the call to the "last, best West."

who had not experienced the fury of a summer storm on the prairie. When he let his team of Clydesdales rest near a fence during a thunderstorm, he saw all six killed by a single bolt of lightning. And when a mountain blizzard sealed a family of German immigrants into their cabin, they learned never to build doors that only opened out.

Western cattlemen learned early how to survive in an extreme climate. A Montana rancher branded 3,747 cattle in the fall round-up of 1886. The mild, dry autumn gave way to continuous snowfalls and minus-fifty degree cold from October to March. When he surveyed his herd the following spring, he found all but 159 steers dead. They had starved and lay in frozen heaps along coulees and riversides. In an attempt to save his herd that same winter, a stockman south of Calgary dragged some of the most exhausted cattle into his ranch

Cowboys on a cattle roundup.

house. He and his wife then tried to revive the animals by pouring warm water over their frozen limbs. Still, losses across the West ranged from twenty to eighty per cent. The winter of 1886 became known as the "Big Die-Up."

In spite of the hardships — treacherous travel, unforgiving climate, and unyielding land — cattlemen still bred stock to build their pilgrim herds, and farmers put another season's promise into the ground. Success would follow. The West was and remains "next year country." Between 1870 and 1880, three million immigrants came to the United States, claiming forty-eight million homestead acres. And in the years from 1896 until the outbreak of the First World War, Canadian promotional propaganda attracted three million newcomers to "the last best west."

Homesteads gave rise to new towns: the town of Vermilion, Alberta, under construction in 1905.

The immigration boom in western North America ended when free or cheap land became real estate, when territory that was once wide open to settlement, became property to be auctioned off to the highest bidder. Once, newcomers from Eastern Europe, Scandinavia, Britain, Quebec, and New England had queued for hours to file for free homesteads. Now there were get-rich-quick land speculators, with promotional literature in one pocket, and land deeds for sale in the other.

Land that had once seemed limitless was now a state or a province. The little that was left sold at a premium. In 1890, when Idaho and Wyoming were admitted as the forty-third and forty-fourth states of the Union, President Benjamin Harrison declared the western frontier closed. Two years later Ellis Island was opened in New York

Branding a steer on the Deer Creek Ranch,
Milk River area, about 1912.

harbor to screen immigrants for the first time, and there was talk of imposing literacy tests before admitting them.

In the young Dominion of Canada, the great western land boom stretched into the twentieth century, but it was the corporate speculators, like the Canadian Pacific Railway, who became the largest landowners. Immigrants were no longer a priority. Some of the best land left was for sale for profit, not offered cheaply to attract the flesh and blood of a nation. A sign of the times was the queue that formed in Edmonton, Alberta, on a night in May, 1912, when 1,500 people waited up to sixteen hours, not to buy land, but simply to take part in a lottery that might allow them to buy it.

The great westward push was over, forever.

The discovery of oil brought new
prosperity and opportunities to the
West: a blow-out circa 1914.

2
The Land:
THE TIMELESS FACE OF THE WEST

It was the great spirit, Wesukechak, who created the lands and waters at the heart of North America, according to some of its first immigrants, the Cree. The task was not an easy one. Wesukechak first had to prove his mettle.

Flood waters had overwhelmed the earth, leaving him and his animal brothers adrift on a raft. For days on end, they searched for dry land.

Finally, in desperation, Nehkik, the otter, retrieved a small piece of mud from beneath the waters. Wesukechak rolled the mud between his hands and blew on it, until the mud became an enormous ball. Putting ashore on this newly-created land mass, Wesukechak set about reshaping the world. He ordered trees and grass to appear. He told Maheekun, the grey wolf, to jump about with his large feet in soft earth to form hollows for lakes, and to push up piles of mud with his nose for mountains. And then he had Misekenapik, the great snake, cut rivers into the earth. And this is how the Cree world was made.

Opposite page:
Cattle browse in a snow-covered pasture near Ridgway, Colorado.

The Cree story of creation has been made mundane by the explanations that geologists have since written. They say that for a million years before the arrival of the native people, the glacial masses of the Quaternay period gripped and gouged the high latitudes of the North American continent. When the climate finally changed, about 14,000 years ago, and the ice was driven northwards by the sun, a vast inland sea was created. It submerged more than 200,000 square miles of territory across what is now the West.

As this glacial ocean retreated, it eroded the western mountain ranges, levelled the central plains and left a web of waterways in its wake. And so glacial action determined the migrations of animal and man, the varieties of vegetation, the means of survival, the patterns of settlement, and the growth of nations. Across the West, the glaciers often sculpted a virtual paradise on earth.

The Rockies are nature's Western masterpiece. They are testament to the powers abroad in that prehistoric period, when fire and water ruled the planet. This string of alpine peaks, linked by meadows and lakes, stretches the length of the West, like a great protruding spine. Long considered obstacles, the Rockies, are in fact, a storehouse of the basics of life. From this range of mountains springs the fresh water for a hundred eastbound rivers — the lifeblood of the Great Plains. Within this alpine chain thrives a cross section of wildlife in its most natural state, preserved today by isolation and man-made sanctuaries — from Yosemite to Jasper. And nestled here are the lush, interior valleys — from the Okanagan in British Columbia, to the Napa in California — that yield the West's bounty of cultivated fruits and vegetables.

Where the Rockies fall to the sea, there lies a coastal environment bearing natural treasures that have drawn generations of immigrants. From the nuggets and flakes of gold beneath the Sierra Nevada, and in the riverbed of the Fraser, to the redwood and fir forests of the northwest, the coastal lands of the West have long been a natural-resource mecca. And east of the Rocky Mountains, the honeycomb of peaks, ice fields, canyons, river sources and salt lakes gives way to the horizontal world of the prairie. The elements — the wild earth, the fire of summer heat, and the floodwaters of spring — are the masters of life here. This great plain, once an inland sea, then the center of the continent, proved to be as great a challenge for man as the mountains. Within its virgin parkland and grassland sod lay the promise of bountiful harvest. But only the will of a dedicated and persistent agricultural society could achieve the fulfillment of that promise in the harvesting of grain and beef.

But the West, so rich in resources, where settlements could take root and prosper — a paradise — also possessed lands that defied survival, that would never be tamed. These were the small kingdoms of the West where Nature reigned supreme.

Between the lush grasslands west of the Mississippi and the foothills teeming with wildlife, lay one such no-man's land — the Badlands — described by General George Custer as "a part of hell with the fires burnt out." In this arid climate of blasting summer winds and winters of frozen darkness, lies a landscape of sagebrush flats, ribbed buttes, capped hoodoos, and the grey-brown clay of a million years' decay. Here only single-minded fossil hunters and grizzled, lone-wolf ranchers survive. Here the mournful howl of the coyote often seems the only signal of life.

Sisters to the Badlands are the deserts of the southwest: the Mojave, Salt Lake, Colorado, and Painted deserts. Here the desolation is complete. It is a land which the novelist, John Steinbeck, called "a mysterious wasteland, a sun-punished place." Most American deserts are treeless. The ubiquitous sagebrush is often the only obvious form of plant life (surviving only because of an oily coating which preserves inner moisture). Vast stretches of these deserts are the salt-and-alkaline remnants of dead lakes, a soil that not even irrigation can redeem. In fact, in 1858, government surveyors from Washington reported to Congress: "The region is altogether valueless. After entering it, there is nothing to do but leave."

And, as if the fire of a merciless sun were not powerful enough to keep Nature sovereign over remote parts of the West, there is also fire and fury underground. For sixty-five million years, two opposing slabs of the earth's crust have pushed at each other beneath the western mountains. This continuous collision has menaced the landscape above for centuries. Where the collision is most intense, molten rock breaks through as volcanic eruptions. Between 1842 and 1857, Mount St. Helens in Washington territory belched fire and ash, then slipped into geological slumber for 123 years. On May 18, 1980, "the Fujiyama of America" exploded with the force of a twenty-megaton nuclear blast, tossing a cubic mile of rock into the sky, chopping to matchsticks every Douglas fir within seventeen miles, killing fifty-nine people, and turning midday as dark as a moonless night with four billion tons of flying ash.

The "rim of fire" that stretches from Japan to New Zealand, from South America to Mount St. Helens in the Cascade Range of the Rockies, has had geological manifestations other than volcanoes to keep civilization at bay. From the moment immigrants arrived west of the mountains to the present day, fifteen major earthquakes have rattled along the San Andreas fault. One of the worst occurred in 1857, in the Tehachapis north of Los Angeles. Another, in 1906, beneath the streets of San Francisco, killed 700. Yet another, in 1971, shook the San Fernando Valley, killing sixty-four. Another is expected before the year 2006.

And yet, as frightening as its nature sometimes appears, the land of the West has always grown peaceful again. After winter blizzards have ended, mountain streams still thaw, and prairie crocuses still bud each spring. When the sun parches the desert, and when dust devils plague the Badlands of the Dakotas and Alberta, the nighttime sky still sparkles with as many stars as the heavens have to offer. And if fire torches coastal brush or mountain forest, the land grows green again, in time.

The landscape of the West changes little from season to season. A jagged mountain skyline may wear smooth in places. Its rivers may meander in a new direction. Sloughs may dot the plains where there were only coulees before. And even man-made incisions may be cut into the earth and rock of its surface. But the personality, strength, and variety of land in the West stays the same.

An uprooted stump stands out
against a wild sky.

Preceding pages:
Wildflowers blossom under
darkening skies: Douglas Ranch,
British Columbia.

Bridge over the Bow River, near
Drumheller, Alberta.

A sign warns of possible obstacles ahead, in southern Arizona.

Following pages: The Fairholme Range of mountains looms above an icy lake in Banff National Park.

Opposite page: A stream tumbles down a boulder-strewn valley in Banff National Park.

The San Juan mountains make a dramatic backdrop to a verdant landscape in Colorado.

Following pages: The Banff Springs Hotel is nestled in the shadow of the Goat Range, Alberta.

An overgrown orchard and a carpet
of flowers in Texas.

A deep blue sky makes the summer
flowers more vivid in northwestern
Colorado.

Freshly-mown hay makes a wave-like pattern near Buena Vista, Colorado.

Opposite page: The historic OH Ranch, near Long River, Alberta, is overshadowed by the soaring Rockies.

The land appears to move toward the sky, in a field near Ramah, Colorado.

Cow hides are draped over the fence on the Ladder Ranch, New Mexico.

A winding road
through the
Rocky Mountains.

Nothing seems to
stir in the Mojave
Desert in daytime.

Preceding pages: Erosion has made "goose necks" out of stone; San Juan River, Utah.

Green and hilly land surrounds a ranch near Lompoc, California.

A white fence bisects the hills on the
Santa Ynez Valley horse ranch,
north of Los Angeles.

Irrigation has made the harsh
country near Montrose, Colorado,
into a rich agricultural region.

A summer storm bears down on
Ridgway, Colorado.

Indian bas-relief on a bridge over the Bow River, near Banff, Alberta.

Hay is provided to the wintering
herd, near Ridgway.

Preceding pages: Dinosaur Provincial Park, Alberta, takes its name from the fossils which have been discovered there.

In Montana it appears that the gold at the end of the rainbow is hay, stacked and stored for winter.

Llamas are not exactly
traditional, but an interesting
alternative to cattle and sheep.

A spectacular view of the Valley Ranch, near Cody, Wyoming.

Opposite page: Coniferous trees dominate the landscape around Emerald Bay, Lake Tahoe, California.

The setting sun makes a fiery sky
over China Lake, California.

Wind, water and frost, acting on
alternate strata of hard and soft
limestone, have made a forbidding
landscape in southwestern Utah.

The Rio Grande is not so grand by late summer, near Las Cruces, New Mexico.

Lake Tahoe, California, occupies a basin more than 6,000 feet above sea level.

Following pages: Ranch buildings are clustered together near Durango, Colorado.

Land of the Big Sky: the view near
High River, Alberta.

The Calgary skyline forms a modern
backdrop to a traditional western
scene.

Horses graze or canter in the lush
Santa Ynez Valley, California.

There is not much barn left, just a roof to cover the hay, in Utah.

Following pages: Day breaks over a western highway.

3
The Life:
MAN AND THE FRONTIER

Opposite page: The foreman of the OH Ranch, Alberta.

When Labor Day, 1912, dawned in Calgary, Alberta, the local newspaper, the *Herald*, published full-page advertisements calling it "the greatest celebration of its kind in the world." By ten o'clock that sunny, September morning, no less than 80,000 citizens lined the streets of this frontier cowtown on the Canadian prairies to witness "the grandest pioneer pageant in all history . . . The Last and Best Great West frontier days celebration."

For the first-ever Calgary Stampede, expatriate American trick roper and promoter, Guy Weadick, had assembled the largest array of original pioneers the West had ever seen. Three thousand Indians led the procession, representing every Western tribe. Among them were a hundred natives from the United States who gloried in parading in full war paint. Hudson's Bay Company factors, missionaries, traders, and even veterans of the original 1874 contingent of the North West Mounted Police followed. American bull trains, prairie schooners, and Red River carts churned up dust onto boardwalks already choked with dazzled onlookers. Spectators included the Duke of Connaught, Governor General of Canada, American artists Charles Russell and Ed Borein, and even vaqueros from Pancho Villa's Mexican bandits. The parade lasted over two hours.

And as the finale to this three-mile-long pioneer pageant, newsreel cameras captured on film more than a thousand hollering horsemen and women — ranch owners, horse wranglers, Hollywood movie cowpunchers, pioneer homesteaders, ranch hands, Mexican rodeo performers, and even fancy riding and roping cowgirls from the cream of the crop of the American wild west shows. While many of them competed for the nearly $16,000 in prize money at the first-ever Frontier Days and Cowboy Championship contest in Calgary, Guy Weadick claimed this was "the sunset of a dying race."

In a sense that first great Stampede was a last tribute to the spirit that had made the old West. Every one of its spectators and participants — whether native descendant of the nomadic tribes which crossed the prehistoric Bering Strait land bridge to North America; East Coast shopkeeper who travelled West by steamboat or prairie schooner in search of his fortune; or European peasant, off the boat at Montreal or New York, who sought refuge from religious persecution, class oppression or starvation, and in pursuit of a homestead — each was an immigrant in a virgin West. Each was a strand in the fabric of pioneer life.

But even as Guy Weadick eulogized "the sunset of a dying race" — the passing of the original pioneers — he was making sure that a way of life in the West was preserved. His Stampede caught on. And just about every year since 1912, at the Calgary Stampede, the Pendleton Roundup, Cheyenne Frontier Days, and the National Finals in Las Vegas, the original cowboy skills of roping, riding, and cowpunching have been featured in rodeo competition.

The first week of every July is cowboy Christmas. In nearly every corral across the West, young jean-clad contestants roll in on pickup trucks, Cessnas, and horse trailers, pay their entry fees and rodeo. They thrive on fast food, beer binges, and Copenhagen chewing tobacco. One will strap himself to the back of a 2,000-pound Brahma bull for eight seconds; another will leap onto a racing steer and wrestle it to the ground; another will rope a dashing calf to a dead stop and pig-tie its legs before the calf knows what hit him. It's a Frederic Remington painting brought to life. It's acting out the John Wayne fantasy. It's a macho test of man against beast — the rodeo cowboy as a North American matador. It's a tradition practised more than 600 times a season, and watched by more than forty million rodeo spectators every year.

Few modern rodeos are staged without an agricultural fair next door. And whether it's the 4-H exhibits, the horse races, or the tractor-pulling contests, the farm tradition today co-exists with the ranching tradition. But this spirit of harmony did not always exist. During the immigrant boom, maverick ranchers refused to concede land to the salt-of-the-earth immigrant farmers. In nineteenth century Wyoming, cattle barons battled settlers over fences, waterholes, and political power. Before the hostilities ended, cattle were rustled and shot, farms razed, and innocents murdered in the crossfire. Eventually, the cattle kingdom was toppled. Trail drives and vast roundups ended. Fences created static ranches and closed-in farmers' fields.

But fences have never assured farm prosperity. When the New York Stock Exchange collapsed in October, 1929, the Depression was already well underway on the farms of western North America. Prices had crashed. Debts had bankrupted 50,000 farmers. But worst of all, on more than 30,000 square miles of the Great Plains, the summers went rainless and the winters, snowless. Winds were blowing away the topsoil. What crops remained, the grasshoppers ate. The Dirty Thirties threatened to turn the bread-basket of the continent into another Sahara desert.

Except that farm people, those tenacious immigrant homesteaders, with their hard-won understanding of agriculture, turned the "dust bowl" around. In western Canada, the farming community created institutions like the Prairie Farm Rehabilitation Administration (PFRA), which built thousands of water-filled dugouts across the prairie. Farmers also benefitted from the work of scientists on experimental farms who developed new strains of hardier grain, and introduced strip farming and tree shelterbelts to fight wind erosion. In the depths of the Dirty Thirties an Alberta farmer named Charles Noble, who had suffered crop failure and the foreclosure of his farm, experimented with a mulching tool to prevent soil erosion. The Noble cultivator came to be used across the continent to preserve prairie topsoils, and ultimately made Charles Noble one of the most successful grain farmers in the West.

Prosperity inevitably follows depression in the West. The boom-

and-bust cycles come and go like the seasons. Oil and gas industry people know the ups and downs better than most. Whether they are taking seismic readings out on a desert while fending off rattlers; roughnecking on rigs in mosquito-infested bush; or making million-dollar decisions in the skyscrapers of Dallas or Calgary; oilmen claim theirs is the last frontier. Sometimes their lives are the stuff of which television soap operas are made, but most often they work in small offices with one phone and a couple of employees. They play a serious game of risk, betting that an investment will cash in on a rich corner of the oil patch. But the biggest thrills in the oil business are experienced in the discovery stage.

In 1930, a determined wildcatter, seventy-one-year-old C.M. "Dad" Joiner, sank his last dollars into a makeshift drilling rig, in a peanut patch in Texas. He struck an oil gusher which opened up the East Texas field — the greatest field ever located in the lower forty-eight United States. That one discovery changed Texas from a rural, agrarian state, to the home of uncounted petroleum millionaires.

Similarly, it was the doggedness of one Vernon "Dry Hole" Hunter, so named for the 133 unproductive wells he had drilled across Saskatchewan and Alberta, before February 13, 1947, that finally paid off. That day in February, his Imperial Oil crew witnessed "a black smoke ring waft out of a flare line," and then the Leduc Number One well blew in, throwing up "a mushroom cloud just like an atomic bomb." "Dry Hole's" oil field soon housed 1,300 wells, containing 200 million barrels of crude. The strike put Leduc Number One and western Canada on the oil industry map, for good.

Many men and women have given the West its place on the map: the wildcatters who made it past the dry wells to the big oil strikes; the farmers who weathered the droughts to plant again; the rodeo competitors who survived the bruises and broken bones to win the "all round cowboy" belt buckles; and all the rest who took up a challenge in the West, either last century or last year. They all share the Western spirit. The pioneers whom Stampede promoter Guy Weadick saw parading into history in 1912 were not the last. The West they migrated to was a young frontier to be shaped by their work and their personalities. The West will always be changed and driven by the lives and thinking of a new generation. The West makes room for pioneer spirit.

A bridesmaid hurries to the door of a pioneer church in Taos, New Mexico.

Following pages: Driving cattle to summer grazing on the Pitchfork Ranch, Wyoming.

Central City, Colorado was a boom town during the gold rush of 1859.

The hired men traditionally slept in log bunkhouses like these, near Cody, Wyoming.

The roads form a curious, honeycomb pattern in Blackhawk, Colorado.

Central City is now a ghost town and tourist attraction.

A big, western-style barn in Big
Horn County, Wyoming.

A weatherbeaten barn provides
imposing shelter for a pair of
roosters, near Buellton, California.

Opposite page: An Indian teepee made for show in the valley of the Shoshone River, Wyoming.

Grain elevators tower above railway cars in Saskatchewan.

Following pages: Some of the crowd awaiting the marchers at the Calgary Stampede Parade.

Farming is a high-tech business,
near Dalhart, in the Texas
panhandle.

Modern, mechanical irrigation in the San Joaquin Valley, California.

Candy-colored chemical tanks brighten a dull horizon, near Dalhart.

Don't look now, but . . . . The big cat peering out at the manager of the Ladder Ranch, New Mexico, is stuffed.

Opposite page: A cowgirl has bloody hands after branding on a British Columbia ranch.

A cat keeps watch outside of an
adobe ranch house in New Mexico.

Sunlight makes the oil lamps shine,
in Skoki Lodge, Banff National Park.

The spirit of innovation is evident at
the annual competition of human-
powered vehicles in Boulder,
Colorado.

An attention-getting
invitation in
Tucson, Arizona.

Portraits on the walls of a New Mexico ranch house keep memories of a pioneering past alive.

Bobcat skins and the skulls of animals decorate the interior of the Ladder Ranch, New Mexico.

Opposite page: Architecture becomes art — Old Faithful Inn, Yellowstone National Park.

Vintage windmill and modern grain
bins on a farm in Powder River,
British Columbia.

Steel silos have replaced wooden
bins on modern western farms.

Above: The harsh climate has scarred both station and vehicle, in East Coulee, Alberta.

Left: Rear wheel steer-ing on a pickup truck in New Mexico.

Right: A pickup truck in Colorado so worn that it blends with the landscape.

Above: Art and commerce side-by-side at a restaurant in Lordsburg, New Mexico.

Opposite page: An Alberta cowboy.

A cowgirl at the Douglas Lake
Ranch, in British Columbia.

The neatly-constructed log corrals
on the Douglas Lake Ranch in
British Columbia.

Root cellars like these made it possible for homesteaders in the northwest to keep vegetables and fruit throughout the long winter.

Flowers adorn the crosses in New Mexico.

Antlers and skulls artistically
arranged over the porch of a
restaurant in Buford, Wyoming.

A street corner in
Blackhawk,
Colorado.

All modern conveniences and refreshments are offered at this New Mexico restaurant.

Soft-drink signs compete for attention on the sun-baked exterior of a southwestern cafe.

R. A. BROWN CATTLE CO.

Bullseyes and near-misses are
recorded on an unhappy
bovine portrait.

Neon at nightfall: a view of
Tonopah, Nevada.

Above: A Texas roadside cafe advertises its fare.

Left: The letter "M" has nodded off at the Driftwood Otel.

Above: Customers are encouraged to linger on the porch of a Colorado cafe.

Right: A good place to hang your hat, and saddle.

Above: The sign points the way to Western history.

Right: A consumer complaint made public in Wyoming.

Opposite page: The gas pump is as old as the station.

Tobacco was once standard cowboy
equipment, as the sign in
Blackhawk, Colorado suggests.

The modern hitching post:
horsepower halted in a western
parking lot.

A western motel provides a stable environment for travellers.

Before television, the library brought civilization to the frontier.

Cows and calves graze peacefully on
the Siggins Ranch, Wyoming.

A branding party
takes a rest in the
Cariboo country
of British
Columbia.

Above and opposite page:
Texas longhorns.

Cattle drive in Wyoming.

Two steers lock horns.

Opposite page:
A youthful cowboy sits tall in the saddle, on a cattle drive in Wyoming.

Ten men watch or hold the patient while one administers treatment on the Douglas Lake Ranch.

Cowboys chivvy the horses along,
near Douglas Lake, British
Columbia.

A rough-hewn fence frames a cattle drive in Wyoming.

Following pages: Low-lying hills and open prairie near Coronation, Alberta.

A natural amphitheater in
Colorado has been the scene of
concerts by John Denver,
among others.

Modern cowboys ride the range on
motorbikes — or race them at
highly competitive meets.

Vehicles are not welcome on the
Valley Ranch, near Cody, Wyoming.

Inside the San Julien Ranch near
Lompoc in southern California.

The deluxe version of the horse trailer.

Equipment for playing polo: Big Horn, Wyoming.

The highway rest stop in Utah
provides shelter from the sun.

The horse waits patiently while the
farrier fits new shoes near Buford,
Wyoming.

Cowboys branding cattle: the Goose
Lake Cattle Company, Bow River,
Alberta.

Refreshments are served in the tent
pitched for a branding party near the
Bow River.

Portrait of the foreman, Ladder
Ranch, New Mexico.

The view from an abandoned ranch
house, Powder River, Wyoming.

Universal symbols of the new west:
pickup and dog.

The rack is for drying hay: Gang
River, British Columbia.

Modern irrigation makes arid land
fertile on the Douglas Lake Ranch,
British Columbia.

A cattle drive cast in bronze
commemorates western history.

The moon shines brightly over
Nogales, Arizona, near the Mexican
border.

ACKNOWLEDGMENTS

All photographs are by Dudley Witney, with the following exceptions:

C. Forsman: 2-3, 42-43, 66-67, 73, 90, 91, 111 (top), 113, 114 (top and bottom), 128, 129, 133, 143 (and back cover).

Roger Witney: 28, 30-31, 34-35, 48, 50-51, 89, 96 (top), and 110.

Glenbow Museum, Calgary, Alberta: 8, 11, 12, 13, 14, 15, 16, 17, 18, and 19.